Sheila,

Have fun in
life and know
that God loves
you.

Brian M. O'Neill

It's The
Drain Your Brain
Ahhhh, and
Bend Your Glasses
Book of Poetry

Brian M. O'Neill

authorHOUSE®

AuthorHouse™
1663 Liberty Drive, Suite 200
Bloomington, IN 47403
www.authorhouse.com
Phone: 1-800-839-8640

First published by AuthorHouse 4/15/2009

ISBN: 978-1-4389-4171-4 (sc)

Printed in the United States of America
Bloomington, Indiana

This book is printed on acid-free paper.

ACKNOWLEDGEMENTS

I would like to thank my family for being supportive and inspirational of my poetry. I would also like to thank The League of American Poets for their encouragement after having published my first poem entitled "Father to Son" (September 11, 2005 included in this book). I would like to also thank God for giving me this gift to express my thoughts, so that people might share a special moment with a stranger, friend, or someone they love.

Table of Contents

FATHER TO SON

A vision of what someday could come to me,

A child into boyhood, now man is what I see.

Knowledge, wisdom, and experience I give to thee,

A reflection of what was and what will be.

My journey was started and now well traveled,

Yours is beginning, not paved but graveled.

Your thirst for the unknown, a constant quest,

Heart felt answers, I give you my best.

Pride, love, never ending care,

Respect, dignity, and passion to spare,

I see in you now what I saw in the beginning,

A proud father, love never ending.

The Stallion

Fragile, small, and struggling to stand,

Glazed at birth, premiers a coat to be grand,

His strides petite, soon become immense,

Prominent movement, his muscles now tense.

Now matured, defined by beauty and grace,

Among his peers, he boldly takes his place.

His majestic mane flawless in the wind,

Mares take notice while being dinned.

His freedom is his power,

His strength forces other colts to cower.

Leader of the herd is left to the mare,

The stallion now protects with dramatic flare.

THE JOURNEY

Tranquility a place I wish to know,

I heard its splendor puts on quite a show.

I've searched high and low but nowhere is it found,

Then a whisper told me to find the thorns of a crown.

I walked for days in search of this majestic piece,

While on my journey another voice was telling me that I must cease.

Determined to finish what I had started I moved onward once again,

As time moved forward, I suddenly realized,
I was back where I began.

Confused I closed my eyes and sought the light,

Steadfast I conquered the fear of the night.

An image of life now radiant with sound,

He came to me and my peace was found.

Understanding

A communication that is received,

The response says it wasn't perceived.

Frustration sets in with the sender of words,

Listen more carefully to the expressions now heard.

Talking to someone is a simple task,

A compassionate person, now to ask,

Living in a world where understanding is a must,

Relationships are built from a foundation of trust.

Years pass by, and insight to loved one does begin to diminish.

As memories slip away, failed communications need to finish.

Intuitive and attention are like intricate pieces of a band,

When spliced together the resolution is to understand.

My Day

A bright light slowly rises from the east,

Time to get started, but first I must feast.

My hunger laid to rest, now it's time to begin,

A fond farewell with a hug and a kiss, and it's off to the den.

The morn slowly passes with the peak of the sun,

A quick break for food, no time to stop, I'll get it on the run.

After a long day of work the sun begins to set,

A long ride home as I've stopped for every light I met.

Finally through my doors with smiles and kisses for one and all,

Now it's time to freshen up before the famous supper call.

Now at last relaxing and enjoying those I love,

Remembering before I sleep, to give Him thanks from above.

WINTER

A chill in the air that makes the body quake,

The night seems to linger, how long will it take?

Soon a white blanket nestles the ground,

Looking through the window fresh tracks are found.

Children build snowmen and sled down great hills,

From dawn until dusk we gaze at their thrills.

Plants lie dormant, no longer in bloom,

Animals gather food and place it in their storage room.

Snow mixes with wind and blizzards are born,

Weathered life is slowly fading, a time to mourn.

A season of change, a time to reflect,

Nature's way of cleansing I've come to expect.

PAINTING A PICTURE

An idea, or a thought, pictured in the mind,

Transferring that image to art, a tedious grind,

The background covered once, a shade to recall,

Different colors selectively added, large and small.

A blot here and a dash there,

The depth now finished with none to spare.

Shapes magically appear, pure clarity,

Impressions now glow with extreme severity.

Stepping back for a moment, a last second glance,

Inspecting for imperfections, leaving nothing to chance,

A coarse cloth fixed to a frame,

The portrait a masterpiece, they will exclaim.

Oceans of Wonder

A bath of blue, as ever seen,

Splendors of coral colorful and green,

Nature's water world of parks,

Filled with excitement, adventure, and terrifying sharks.

The tides are high and the tides are low,

As the wind picks up, it's a white cap show.

A diversity of life can be found in this wonderland,

The performers vary, from microscopic to those oh so grand.

The ocean is full of mystery and adventure for all to share,

You can traverse through hundreds of dwellings if you dare.

A world that remains in constant motion,

Great experiences await when you visit the ocean.

MIDDLE OF THE ROAD

Clarity: The ability to see with clearness, what you see.

As we travel through life we most often find ourselves in harmony, and

in control while heading in the right direction.

Just up the road there's a bend, or is it a T-intersection, or better still

a simple fork in the road.

Life's challenges are appearing constantly before us.

It use to be so simple, but now we must think faster than we ever

did, even though we want to slow down.

Which direction do we take left or right?

Emotions run high, as our hearts pound with joy and fear.

Close encounters of the human kind, looking for their special road.

Every so often we find ourselves on the straight and narrow only

To be blind-sighted because of what we failed to see or chose not to.

There we are in the middle of the road, uncertain what to do.

What do we let drive us, mind, heart, feelings, instinct, or all of these?

We pray for guidance and await His call.

MY INSPIRATION

I see her giving endlessly in passion and care
Even to those not willing to share
Her faith in love shared by all, yet given to one
Helping hands always, till the work is done

She devotes her time and energy to three
The Father, the work, and her family
Even in times of distress and despair
Grace comes from her, all receiving repair

By God's blessing she was born into this world
Received by the Holy Spirit, now unfurled
A vision of love and compassion, even in death
My love for her eternal, beyond my last breath

My New Born Rose

Life from your mother with a shout of expression,

announcing that you had awaken,

My eyes met yours and my heart was taken.

Tiny and frail, yet you looked so grand,

Even as you blossomed and learned how to stand.

Now you've learned to speak and you spoke your mind,

Always straight forward, honestly, truthfully,

and remembering to be kind.

Exploring your passions you began new quests,

Doubting at times, guessing at others,

but always giving it your best.

A lady transformed you have come to be,

From a sprouting bud into the perfect rose is what I see.

From start to present I've cherished your growth,

A proud father forever I thank God for you both.

FORGIVENESS

Inflicting pain on another and the hurt runs deep,

A word is spoken in haste that someone quickly regrets.

False accusations without seeking the truth,

Denying the facts, such that lies have become reality,

Finally caught in a web of deceit,

Humbled and humiliated by that which has been done.

Asking for forgiveness begins the slow process of recovery.

Vowing to never repeat the event again,

People working together to find a solution,

A broken heart is mended by grace.

No longer traveling the same pathway, but finding peace,

Hope, faith, love, three things our Father taught us to share.

LOVE

Love is the word that captivates the human mind and heart.

It is four letters put together that can create an explosive impact.

It is sometimes expressed through alternative methods.

It use to have a true meaning, a strong bond, which meant desire

and passion for someone.

Now the word seems to have lost some of its purpose, befallen for a

means of necessity.

Love is a word that makes the heart beat with intense contractions of
joy,

or when taken away inflicts a magnitude of pain.

Love is a word most frequently shared in times of heavenly bliss, or

sadly forgotten in times of broken dreams.

Love is a word that has become second nature to most, however still

remains sacred to a few.

Love is a powerful word that has the strength to create an affection

shared by all.

Love is a word that only the user gives its meaning to.

THE SONG

It starts with the intake of air,

While the throat relaxes the eyes just stare.

Slowly exhaling through the mouth,

Sound flows outward in all directions, north, east, west, and south.

Words are now heard with a different twist,

A harmony of notes now exists.

The melody sung with passion and flare,

Expressions of joy are now what we share.

The singer now stands in front of the crowd,

The applause starts low but grows very loud.

The words have been spoken and the message was sent,

The performance now over and away he went.

THE TEACHER

The foundation of life comes with education,

Striving to give those we love our gratification.

Learning blocks mastered, while comprehending a new skill,

Giving back to those who gave, oh what a thrill,

Nurturing the best of all that is learned,

Finding someone who can teach, that's what's yearned.

There once was a Teacher, who said it best,

"Abide by my Father's rules and you will surely pass His test".

Many have tried, few have succeeded, and most have failed.

A readjustment, a heartfelt decision, the new boat has sailed,

Our spirits free, His chosen student is now preaching,

His school is always open, for He is always teaching.

My Star

It is bright up there in the still of the night,

Like a beacon from above flashing its radiant light.

It never wanders too far from me,

While sometimes it is hidden and very hard to see.

It often has a few close friends which band near it,

This has led some to give them names by which they're now a hit.

My star has no special name, just a term of direction,

It is in that word that when I'm lost I find my sole protection.

Once a year my star takes center stage across the earthly lands,

It sits atop an evergreen held tightly in a stand,

My star now fades into the light as if to say good-bye,

I know my star will soon return as I peek into the sky.

A MYSTERY

A puzzling scenario with all kinds of twists,

Formulating what happened now persists.

Solving the unknown, a thirst some desire,

Accomplish this feat, and others will admire.

A riddle that provokes the thought process,

Interpreting facts that will surely confess,

Misdirection, the ultimate object in a great mystery,

Sleuths renowned can be found, while looking back on history.

A situation to ponder, or one to decide,

Resolution versus the unexplained, two worlds that collide,

Deciphering the phantom perplexity is not always attained.

Determined diligence however, is always to be maintained.

CHRISTMAS

Jingle bells, sleigh rides, Christmas trees, and mistletoe,

Pure white snow, angels on high, and presents of many sizes,

A time of surprises, giving, sharing, and loving,

Memories of the past and those created now.

Three kings bearing gifts following a star,

The birth of our Savior where straw and animals lay,

Voices singing songs that lift our spirits,

We celebrate on high with a festive feast.

A time of grace and opening our hearts,

The thought that counts, not the size of the package,

The giving of hope to those in need,

A peace shared by all, as united we live in harmony.

THE CHRISTMAS PRESENT

The anticipation of seasonal bliss, with an exchange,

A sacred moment, packaging then decorate, now to arrange,

Crimson wrapped with ribbons of gold,

Topped with a bow, breath-taking to behold,

Pristine in dimensions, as it lay beneath the tree,

Though surrounded by others it stands alone in beauty.

Inside this package a heartfelt gift,

Thoughts within it will surely uplift.

Writing on the card explains a little more,

Unveiling this package, now down to the core,

Overwhelmed with joy and expressing gratitude,

Love and grace are forever renewed.

MARRIAGE

It started with a courtship, where love had just begun,

The union of two souls, the bonding into one,

Walking down the aisle to make those sacred vows,

Statements of commitment and all they endowed.

Accepting this to be the ultimate invitation,

Proclaiming your devotions before God's Holy station,

Keeping fresh in your minds what brought you together,

This will be the glue that holds you both forever.

Sacrifices made on behalf of the one you cherish,

Selfless acts that promote the marriage to flourish,

Attentively listening to each others words,

Understanding nurtures this heavenly bliss upwards.

PRAYER

I pray to God speaking from my heart,

My words are honestly spoken from the very start.

I know He will listen intensely to what I have to say,

He never interrupts me, even if it takes all day.

My conversation with Him can be held anytime and any place,

I may not physically see Him, but I'll always receive His grace.

I sometimes pray not for myself, but for that of troubled others,

The bible says no matter where we're from we are all bonded brothers.

My confession now given to my Father from above,

Anxiously I wait to receive His spiritual love.

I know He's always with me even when I stray,

To find my way back I simply need to pray.

Senses/Expressions

Sight: To see the wonders of the world, to see you.

Eyes that reveal a longing for understanding,

and which tell of happiness and sorrow.

Visions of what is, what could've been, and what will be.

Hearing: To listen, absorb, and comprehend the sounds of life.

The sound of your voice, that of joy and sadness.

A soft spoken word that says I care, I love you, or I'll be there.

Silence says anger, frustration, or I no longer care.

Touch: To embrace that which we yearn for, you and I together.

To reach out and receive, as well as, say what we're afraid, unsure,

or in need of.

Taste: The fruits of life that fill our hunger, the essence of love

which drives all creations.

Unfilled it leaves an emptiness, a lifeless spectacle.

Smell: An aura which aids in guiding our actions,

which ultimately lead to our detection of persecution, or ecstasy.

THE EAGLE

Majestic in stature from high above,

Vibrant feathers display its pride.

Boldly encompassing its crown and tail, pure glory,

Sounds of authority flow freely from its throat.

Razor like talons with grips of steel,

Soaring through the sky with elegance and beauty,

Scoping the countryside with vision so keen,

Endangered and protected, diligently studied and enjoyed.

Symbolic to some while honored by others,

A national treasure found on a variety of facets.

Flown from a standard, liberty shouts out loud,

Freedom reigns supreme for his majesty.

HALLOWEEN

This ghostly day was brought about by people known as Celts,

Their costumes made of animal heads and their pelts.

The Romans came along and added a different kind of twist,

Thanks to them the tradition of "bobbing" for apples now exits.

It has been called "The Festival of the Dying Year".

When ghouls and goblins scare us, as they shriek and sneer.

Many traditions have been handed down from our ancient past,

The myth of "Jack O'Lantern" for example, remains steadfast.

Then there's the carving of that large orange-colored fruit,

It has a variety of faces, some aren't quite so cute.

Traditional dressing up in various types of garments,

Then there's trick-or-treating while receiving tasteful presents.

THE WHISPER

Hearing a voice peacefully speaking in the night,

Looking around, but finding no one in sight.

A message so faint yet crystal clear,

Now attentive and alert for someone is near.

Pondering a response to the messenger's voice,

Actions were dictated, following a choice.

Soft spoken sounds flowing gently into the atmosphere,

Grasping and translating brings a smile, opposed to a sneer.

Whispers of logic and sound advise,

Sometimes however the words are not so nice.

Communicating quietly while intently taking notice,

Understanding with reservation, is it fact or is it bogus?

Who Am I

Born into this world I struggle to find myself, my place, and my purpose for being.

One day I awaken to find that I exist, but where am I? Strange noises around me arouse my curiosity.

A constant image of one who watches over me makes me feel secure and then teaches me of life and its choices.

I search to find the true meaning of what I've been taught.

My decisions are those of trial, error, and corrections. My journey now becomes one of finding myself and how I fit into this mystic puzzle we call life.

Now I must pursue that quest that I long for, in hope that once I've found it I'll become whole.

A guiding light shows me how I must begin, yet caution seems to steer my footsteps along the way.

Occasionally tripping or falling down I find the way to right myself and continue

Often finding myself in the company of others, who have traveled my path, gives me the strength to find my door and unlock my identity.

THE BIKE

Smooth, lined, or rugged, they all grip the ground,

Radial lines help keeping them round.

The magnificent frame resting on those hubs,

Aligning wheels into the forks, assuring neither rubs.

The crank arm provides the means to movement,

Supplying power to the pedals is often not so pleasant.

Guiding this machine are things called handlebars,

Knowing how to steer and brake will prevent those nasty scars.

Padding on the seat, especially for long rides,

Conserve the energy when possible, always down hillsides.

Economically sound, while providing a way to stay in shape,

It's the ultimate mode of travel when you just want to escape.

MORALITY

Things we're taught at a precious age,

Soon become our actions as we enter center stage.

One person fails where another succeeds,

Decisions are made on wants and needs.

Values which prosper and those that fade,

While promises are broken and new ones are made.

A sense of right and that, which is wrong,

Some reactions are quick while others are too long.

Morals are like flowers we plant to bloom,

Nurturing them first and later we'll groom.

Standards we live by that help us to grow,

In the end, we'll be judged by our deeds, not what we know.

I Love You

I see – but am blind to you,

I listen – but cannot hear you,

I understand – but fail to change,

I seek – but do not find,

I walk – but do not move,

I cry – but shed no tears.

Strength comes from prayers,

Forgiveness brings understanding,

God brings life, you bring love,

The path I follow in the future,

brings togetherness, vision, sound, and harmony.

CHURCH

A house for worship, a house for praise,

A place the shepherd speaks Holy words, while we listen and graze.

A place to receive forgiveness, when God's laws have been broken,

A place we share fellowship with many words spoken.

A majestic place with beauty, grace, and serenity,

It's the house where you find the Holy Trinity.

A place whose doors are opened to all walks of life,

It's a house where unions are made between husband and wife.

A place where christening new life is a joy to see,

A place I long for and always want to be.

Church is the one place you can find the one true Boss,

The place you'll find our true Savior, Jesus Christ, upon the cross.

VALENTINE

This act of love which is displayed,

So very often has flowers arrayed.

Affection shown with inviting blends,

Cupid eyes his target, while his bow slowly bends.

That time of year when romance hits new peaks,

When the mouth is silent and the heart is the one who speaks.

Chocolates, flowers, and cards, favorite "Ole Time" customs,

These remembered thoughts speak with volumes.

Inspirations of passionate view,

Reflective moments we must pursue,

A day we celebrate Saint Valentine,

Reminiscing romantic love, be it forever enshrined.

THE WALL

It happens when you speak, or sometimes by actions you take,

Never to be seen, but always disrupting choices you make.

It may be small or very tall, an impassable block,

Soon the sides join in as they begin to flock.

You try to go over, under, and around but fail,

Frustrated and saddened you begin to wail.

Out of nowhere comes a voice, a light of hope,

You listen intently and then give thanks for the life saving rope.

Looking your wall straight in the face you say "I'm ready",

Your steps shaky at times, while the helping hand keeps you steady.

You've broken down that hard cast shell,

Two hearts now open and caring as well.

THE DISCIPLE

What did he learn as a child in the house of God?

Like a good shepherd He will lead us with a rod.

Treat others with respect as you would have them treat you,

Never be ashamed of the work that you do.

A young boy's vision to help change the world,

His dreams of what he can do now become swirled.

Foresight of glamour and what someday could be,

He works hard for his respect, honor, and glory for all to see.

The boy transformed to man begins his direction in life,

Knowing there will be plenty of mystery and strife.

All for God's glory is what he keeps in mind,

The fruits of his labor he will ultimately find.

THANKSGIVING DAY

Our forefathers celebrating a harvest festival,

A reciprocal event that's most often tribal.

A variety of side dishes accompany the main prize – turkey,

To include potatoes, pies, corn, and a sauce made of cranberry.

As a substitute, goose or duck may represent the main dish,

A missing furcula bone leaves no grant to a wish,

A day first generation immigrants inspired a historical parade,

One that features the "Jolly Old Elf", who's always hurrahed,

A day even football competes with "Mans' Best Friend".

The A.K.C. will crown the one canine who transcends.

A formal proclamation made by the first president,

It promotes the unity of people with a heartfelt movement.

PATIENCE

P	Pause before any action you take,
A	Acceptance of the decisions you make.
T	Trusting you made the right choice,
I	Interpreting the words from your voice.
E	Exercise good judgment in what you've done,
N	Nourishing calmness until there is none.
C	Controlling your emotions before you act,
E	Expressions of love is what you extract.

Patience is a virtue we all wish to obtain,

Patience is a gift not so easy to maintain.

MOM

You gave birth to me with joyful tears,

Tending my health needs through the years,

Knowledge and grace you've given to me,

Now I practice those gifts for all to see.

Your heart as big as the galaxies above,

You constantly give your bountiful love.

Endless strength beyond compare,

Your style and beauty has its own kind of flair.

A mother will always hold a special place in each son's heart,

Bonded at birth, joined forever, they'll never be far apart.

A mother's work is never done, just too much to do,

Mom, all I have to say is, "I love you".

KNOWLEDGE

I want to know why people grow,

I want to know what makes it snow.

I want to know how planes can fly,

I want to know why blue is the color of the sky.

Knowledge they say is best learned at play,

Knowledge for others is learned while in school from August till May.

Some will say knowledge is passed down from the generation before,

While others will say knowledge is found in the history store.

Webster state's knowledge is learning,

Intelligence, wisdom, theories, and philosophy keep us yearning.

Knowledge is a constant evolution of the mind,

Information unlimited we seek and we find.

Building a Bridge

Life is so simple and pure from the beginning of birth.

Time passed and the simple became complex with new challenges.

The budding child had now grown to maturity.

You looked for that magical world you read about in books,

Only to find that it really wasn't where you thought it might be.

Then one day you found it,
the place you had searched for, or had you?

At first your heart ran wild with excitement, those tears were for joy,

and your laughter spoke of happiness.

Now that flame that once burned bright in your heart has begun to dim.

Your tears now show the pain you bare.

Your laughter now a means to forget and escape,

that which you once believed in.

In times of suffering you pray for guidance from Thee who can heal.

You don't know how, or where the strength, or when help will come.

Your road seems to have come to a dead end.

Unsure of what to do next you start to leave the road,

down into the valley of regret, from which few return.

You start to step and suddenly realize that you haven't fallen

off the road, instead your now standing on a bridge of choice.

This new bridge of hope gives you means to find that which you desire.

A Birthday Party

There's going to be a birthday, so how does one prepare?

The party so creative and dynamic, no others will compare.

The cake made to order, one with lots of style,

Lighted candles on this pastry are sure to get a smile.

A list to make of those helping share this festive day,

Invitations to those guests send them right away.

The special day arrives, as do the invited friends,

Bearing cards and gifts, a "Happy Birthday" each one extends.

Sharing this time with those so dear in heart,

There is laughter, joking, and love until they depart.

On rare occasions a surprise party will be planned,

Keeping this a secret will come with great demand.

A Rainbow to Remember

Darkened sky, crooked electricity seen from afar,

Pounding thunder not quite so bizarre,

The sky clears, an awesome sight to behold,

Seven brilliant rays have begun to unfold.

Nature's way of emitting a colorful show,

Aligned to perfection in their rows,

An optical situation as the sunbeams shine,

A spectrum of rays has been designed.

Short lasting, its eminent beauty will ultimately fade.

Legend has, at the end of it, wealth is portrayed,

An arch that leads to the golden treasure,

A mystic quest only a leprechaun will pleasure.

BROKEN RHYME

Bones in pools, carts can roam,

Cones are stools, darts can't foam.

Phones have rules, hearts are home,

Tones cry mules, parts of a poem.

Backs have fins, hose by hand,

Packs with bins, pose goes the band.

Sacks of pins, rows in a stand,

Racks made of tins, toes in sand.

Chairs by cars, boats on blocks,

Stairs in bars, floats like rocks,

Hairs on jars, notes on clocks,

Flares of stars, quotes on stocks.

INTO THE LIGHT

The night has fallen and I feel all alone,

Silence fills the air while I sit here in my home.

I listen to the wind as it howls outside my door,

Tiny little drops and then the all out pour.

Light begins to flash and then I hear the boom,

Now darkness falls everywhere along with its gloom.

I feel my heart pounding as panic seeps in,

I close my eyes and see Him as my prayer slowly begins.

As quickly as it started the disturbance now is calm,

Light now penetrating the darkness as my hand is held in His palm.

Peace fills my mind as the Holy Spirit enters,

Now knowing God is my one true center.

SUNDAY

They call it the Sabbath, a day of rest.

Religious beliefs, a time God hears what we've confessed.

The seventh day of a calendar week,

It's a day for reflection and critique.

The period of time between Saturday and Monday,

A month beginning on Sunday has a Friday the 13th, by the way.

Old English states it means "day of the sun,"

Christians call it the "Lords Day," come all ye brethren.

Once a year this day brings out football fanatics,

While we listen to announcements become super critics.

Along side the traditional egg hunt, with minimal guidance,

It's the day of resurrection, a time of festive remembrance.

The Trial

There once was a man, noble and pure,

He spoke from the heart, becoming the cure.

A person of passion, love, and care,

One who gave His all, even to those in extreme despair.

A man with visions shared by most,

For they came to be with Him from coast to coast,

Some thought Him supreme, while others said "A fraud of sort".

Afraid of His words, they scourged Him before the court.

Guilty of nothing He bore our sins,

His death on a cross, our salvation begins.

Expressions of thanks from all of us,

We proclaim and glorify the name Jesus.

DADDY'S GIRL

A God sent bundle of heavenly bliss,

Her framework so fragile, a soft gentle kiss,

Eyes that melt even the coldest of hearts,

Nimble fingers that never let us part,

Like a rose in the spring you slowly begin to bloom.

Infancy into childhood, now you loom,

Fantasy into reality, now standing on your own,

Joyful tears, playful smiles, endless love forever shown.

Now comes the time I dread the most,

From father to mentor, no longer your host,

A loving embrace, a kiss for luck, with memories to spare,

Now comes your time and all that you share.

I'm Afraid

I heard it said that anyone who is not afraid is a fool,

In today's world too many people are just mean and cruel.

I'm afraid of hatred and the loss of trust,

I see people with little to no patience and violence as a must.

I'm afraid world peace will be a constant crusade,

People with closed minds and cold hearts are not easy to persuade.

I'm afraid family values have hit a wicked slippery slope,

I'm afraid of people losing all sense of hope.

I'm afraid of failing and hurting those I love,

I'm afraid of never entering the kingdom that's above.

I'm afraid of growing old and watching memories fade,

My God has told me to believe and have faith, and never be afraid.

OUR CHILDREN

They laugh and play while making us smile,

At the park they swing, hang, and slide into the sand pile.

Energy to burn with some to spare,

Hours of joy are what they share.

Questions are plenty as they try to figure things out,

Overwhelmed at times, mom and dad just want to shout.

Children give us a glimpse of our past,

We try to savor it knowing it won't last.

Our children soon blossom into a nurturing class,

Life gives them new challenges, we hope they will pass.

Our youngsters soon marry and have children of their own,

As grandparents we hope they continue to

flourish, with all they've been shown.

THE CALM BEFORE THE STORM

I see, I watch, I wait, and prepare for what I know is destine.

The serenity of your life so apparent,

Yet an air of darkness looms on the horizon.

Your heart was given to one who pledged an eternity of love.

Time passes as does the clarity of your union of bliss.

Clouds, not forecasted, begin to slowly develop

And create moderate turbulence in your life.

Concerns are expressed, however not all seem to be concerned,

With the darkness that is slow to enclose them.

Disregard for the warning signs of the past bring a darkness,

Which is briefly brightened by visions of events yet to happen?

Exchanges made with violent consequences to all.

Damage done, repair not an option, the rebuilding will be slow.

Who do you trust, believe in, share with, care for, and learn to love?

I'll be there.

THE GAME

I want to play it but don't know how,

Can you help me? I really want to understand it now.

The rules are complex and will take time to learn,

Patience and practice I must apply for they are stern.

I give it a try but find it hard at first,

Failure only heightens my determination and thirst.

To master the skills is what I have in mind,

Conquering them is not as easy as I will find.

My success will likely come somewhere down the road,

Experience you see is the secret to this code.

Zeal and zest are reasons why I play the game,

For if not these reasons, then truly I think it's a shame.

The Tree

Booming in stature with a canopy providing shade,

From a sapling it's grown into the greatest colossal ever made.

Buds a bloom come early spring,

Song birds soon follow and sing, sing, sing.

Now comes summer and the tree is a ripen green,

Its leaves have many shapes and sizes, and some not even seen.

Autumn brings a scenic change,

As beauty blends into a colorful range,

While temperatures drop the leaves slowly depart from its arms,

A barren of bark, no longer a brilliance of charm,

As winter passes through the forest grows anew,

Seedlings begin to sprout with each morning dew.

61

Time to Age

Tick tock, tic tock, tic tock,

Time keeps moving, the biological clock.

The sun rises and the sun sets with each passing day,

Your body quakes as you begin to rise and play.

Youthful years where fear has no place,

Then change comes about, in the mirror we see our face.

Our body's have gone from new to used,

Then one day we realize, they're worn out having been abused.

The days of fast and graceful movements have passed us by,

Turtle's we've become, energy faded, and quite often very shy.

Observing life differently now, having left center stage,

Once, time seemed like eternity now it discharges us with age.

Printed in the United States
145260LV00005B/19/P